Spices Mixes 101: Seasoning Cookbook

The Ultimate Guide To

Mixing Spices & Herbs

Table of Contents:

Introduction

Introduction

We like to be surrounded by all kinds of scents, colors and tastes – and there is no greater joy than to share our experience with others!

Spices are those substances that improved the quality of food preparation for millennia, and that continue to fascinate and create the true taste of gourmet cuisine in different nations.

The borders of culinary culture are difficult to pass. But not impossible!

What would a tasty meal for the modern man be, if it were deprived by these delicacies that intoxicate the senses and tempt the taste? Currently, we are witnessing a massive expansion of them in all social spheres, because, with the development of industry, trade and transport, endless pursuit of these "miracle foods" has ended, as they became available very easily all over the world.

Once accessible only to the very wealthy, spices were a very strong trading currency between nations. Today, the existence of the abundance of spices seems normal. But things were a lot different in the past.

The discovery and history of spices – A fascinating story

History of spices and herbs began soon after the appearance of man. Manuscripts relating to the use of spices dated back more than 5,000 years. Traditional Chinese medicine is based on mixtures of plants and Hippocrates himself used them for medicinal purposes. In ancient Greece plants were dedicated to the Gods.

The spices were so greatly desired by the people that it affected the course of history.

Road spices probably started in China, Indonesia, India or Ceylon. Chinese traders were the first who sailed to the Spice Islands (now Maluku, a group of islands in Indonesia) and brought loads of spices and perfumes by Indian or Ceylon coast, where Arab traders were waiting for them. Arabs have long hidden the sources of flavored goods, but also the roads that could reach up to these exotic places. A classic route would be to cross the river Indus by the Pesharwar through to the Khyber Pass, through Afghanistan and Iran, then south to the city of Babylon on the Euphrates. The spices were brought there by the most powerful cities and towns of the day. The Phoenicians, great navigators and traders, prospered by trading spices and even established a large distribution centre in the city of Tyre, which served throughout the Mediterranean. Their golden era was from 1200 to 800 BC.

As centres of power moved from Egypt to Babylon and Assyria, the Arabs continued to hold control over the sources of spices from the East and flowering during Greek and Roman civilizations.

The Romans were also great lovers of spices and seasonings. The high demand on the market made it necessary to find a way to India, to break the Arab monopoly on the spice trade. But it was not long until the Roman ships loaded with precious spices started sailing towards Alexandria, Egypt's main port.

Romans used spices in cooking; they scented their rooms with spice threads and oils made from spices as perfume for their and bath lamps. Wherever their legions marched, they brought with them the richness of spices, being the first to wear exotic flavors to northern Europe.

The downfall of the Roman Empire in the fifth century, the dawn of the Dark Ages and the disruption of migratory people meant a long period of stagnation in many areas, including that of merchants of spices.

Ancient writings tell us that Muhammad, the founder and prophet of the Muslim religion, married the widow of a rich merchant of spices.

From the Bible we learn that the Queen of Sheba travelled from her native Ethiopia, to visit King Solomon in Jerusalem, and was impressed by his wisdom and wealth which, amongst others, came from trading of spices and the gifts he received: "All those seeking to listen to the wise words (of Solomon) always brought expensive gifts and spices". (Kings, 10:25)

Prophet Joseph's story has also been in connection to the trade in spices. His brothers were jealous and had decided to kill him, but a group of Ishmaelites were coming down from Gilead on their camels carrying spices, balm and myrrh, transporting them to Egypt. The brothers sold him for twenty pieces of silver and Joseph returned to their father, Jacob, with bloodstained clothes. Jacob was struck with grief. Finally, Joseph became a high ranking servant of the court. His talent to interpret Pharaoh's dreams saved his adopted country of famine. Later, he took immense satisfaction to sell corn to his brothers, who did not recognize him. Instead they brought him gifts; balm, honey, spices, myrrh, nuts and almonds.

Marco Polo was born in 1256 into a family of merchants who were fascinated by the Orient. They had travelled far and wide in China, they lived at the court of the Mongol King Great Khan, and, during a trip that lasted 24 days, Marco went through China, Asia and India. His story, The Adventures of Marco Polo, was written on parchment during imprisonment after a great battle between Venice and Genoa. His book described the amazing spices which he had seen in his travels. He poetically wrote about Java: "abundant in valuable assets, pepper, nutmeg, cloves; all the spices and herbs are valuable products of the island, which is often visited by vessels of commerce". His book inspired all the seafarers that followed his footsteps, eager to become famous and rich.

The age of discovering new lands in 1400 was just beginning, and the story of spices continues. European seafarers were obsessed with their dream of finding the best (sea travel) route to the Middle East and India. Vasco da Gama, the Portuguese navigator, was the first who discovered the sea route to India through the Cape of Good Hope, the southernmost point of Africa. He was not received with much hospitality, but still managed to load the boat with nutmeg, cloves, cinnamon, ginger and chilli grain. But it was welcomed home as a hero in 1499 and, more importantly, brought a letter from the Indian leaders of Calicut who signed a partnership agreement on spices trading.

Not long after, Lisbon, the capital of Portugal, took over the role of "capital of spices" position, enjoyed so much in the past by Venice.

In 1492, Christopher Columbus thought that he arrived in Japan, but actually he arrived in San Salvador, one of the islands near the Bahamas, Haiti and Cuba. Discovering the New World, he was the first Westerner to taste the chilli burner. On the second trip, Columbus left Spain with 1,500 men to establish the supremacy of the Spanish in the New World, hoping to find gold and oriental spices; instead, he found pepper and vanilla in the great South American continent, and brought potatoes, chocolate, corn, peanuts and turkeys to Europe.

But the Portuguese have made a huge mistake engaging the Dutch as traders, their carriers in Europe, asking them to sail towards the Island of spices to bring cloves, nutmeg and cinnamon. After a century of domination complete, the Portuguese were outdone by the Dutch.

The Dutch East Indian Company, who patronized the spice trade, was established in 1602 in response to the formation of the British East Indian Company, which had been given Royal Charter by Queen Elizabeth I in 1600. Meanwhile, Sir Francis Drake sailed around the world through the Strait of Magellan and crossed the Pacific to the Spice Islands. These islands were coveted throughout Europe, many countries wanting the monopoly on the spice trade, because they knew it was a reliable source of great wealth.

The Dutch tried to restrain the growth of nutmeg and clove to only Amboyna, Banda Islands and in the Moluccas, in which they operated. The plan was thwarted, however, by a French missionary, Pierre Poivre, who found seedlings on a neighboring island, where the seeds were brought by birds, and transported them to Mauritius. Cloves have been carried further, to Zanzibar, which has remained the largest producer to this day, and nutmeg to Grenada, West Indies, also known as the Mace Island.

Around the same time, the British were experimenting with nutmeg and clove plantation in Penang and later cultivated spices in Singapore, under the leadership of Sir Stamford Raffles, a famous employee of East India Company and the founder of Singapore.

The battle between the Dutch and the British became more bitter and bloody, lasting almost 200 years. The conflict was resolved only when the British took over India and Ceylon, and the Dutch took over Java and Sumatra, which remained under their jurisdiction until the Second World War. At that time, the spices had become a commodity much cheaper, which could be found almost everywhere in large quantities.

Late eighteenth century brought another nation on the stage of spice producers: USA. Vessels from New England successfully carried pepper corn. After negotiations and other exchanges, schooners returned to Salem in Massachusetts with huge reserves of the best Sumatran pepper. Salem became the trading centre of pepper and, with a potential profit of 700%, commercial ship owners have become the first millionaires. These trips were not very easy though. The journey took up to two or three years, the possibility of being attacked by pirates or natives was high, not to mention the great storms at sea.

Nowadays, the main places selling spices are London, Hamburg, Rotterdam, Singapore and New York. Spices are checked before being stored in huge warehouses, then they are sold and sent to processing and packaging. Spice trading rises up to million dollars a year. Black pepper is the top of the list, followed by chilli and cardamom. India is the main producer, followed by Indonesia, Brazil, Madagascar and Malaysia. The spices are vital to the economy of these countries.

The most expensive spices today are saffron, followed by vanilla and cardamom.

Superstitions "move" mountains

Along with the old beliefs that emphasized the healing powers of plants, other applications have evolved, applications that do not necessarily have anything to do with human health, namely: the use of plants and spices as aphrodisiacs. It is said that parsley contains essential oils that increase potency in men. The only question refers to the amount plant that must be added to food in order for it to work!

Other spices, such as vanilla, supposedly have an exciting effect due to their flavor, which is similar to human pheromones. This is probably the reason why vanilla is not used in monasteries and convents: in order not to induce an adulterous behavior.

On the strength of the odor that they emanate, other plants are considered aphrodisiacs, such as cardamom and fennel. The substances they contain, especially estragole, make the anise, basil and lemon grass plants also be considered aphrodisiacs.

Other plants that are considered to have aphrodisiac status are saffron, ginger, myrrh, coriander. Ginger, chilli, mustard and cinnamon are other members of the world spices that stimulate the body, mind and soul, not just in an erotic sense.

Spice Mixes and Blends.

Discover a world of authentic flavors, with spices from across the globe.

1. Chilli powder

This is the dried, crumbled fruit of one or more selections of chilli pepper, sometimes with the addition of other spices, like; garlic, oregano, cumin, coriander and cloves.

Chilli powder is sometimes referred as one specific type of chilli pepper used (i.e cayenne pepper), other types of hot pepper may be used, such as; ancho, jalapeño, New Mexico, and pasilla chillies.

Basic recipe:

-2 Tablespoons paprika
-2 teaspoons oregano
-1 1/2 teaspoons cumin
-3/4 teaspoon onion powder
-1 1/2 teaspoons garlic powder
-1/2 teaspoon cayenne pepper (omit or increase to taste)

As a result of the various likely additives, the spiciness of any given chilli powder is variable.

Chilli powder blends are particularly popular in American cuisine, where they are the primary component in chilli con carne.

Chilli powder is a widely used spice in various stews, soups, and -- of course -- chillies. It can also be used as a fundamental element of marinades or dry rubs for meats as well as incorporated into burgers.

Health Benefits:
Chilli powder is actually a wholesome seasoning, it's very healthy for you with significant amounts of several beneficial nutrients.

-Vitamin A
-Vitamin C

2. Curry powder

A spice mix of widely varying combinations based on the South Asian cuisine, but was popularized during the 19th and 20th century in the western world due to the mass exportation of the powder was a used for flavouring food after it was discovered by troops and other colonial visitors in the East. In the mid-20th century, Indian cuisine became popular globally, so curry and thus curry powder, became widely available.

The curry powder blends of up to 20 different herbs and spices, including the commonly used: coriander, turmeric, cumin, fenugreek, and chilli peppers; depending on the recipe, additional ingredients such as ginger, garlic, fennel seed, asafoetida, caraway, cinnamon, clove, mustard seed, cardamom, green cardamom, black, nutmeg, long pepper, and black pepper may also be included. Quality curry powder would also contain curry leaf.

Health Benefits of Curry Powder:

- Reduces Inflammation
- Prevention and Treatment of Cancer
- Protects Against Alzheimer's
- Aids Digestion

Basic recipe:

-2 tablespoons whole cumin seeds, toasted
-2 tablespoons whole coriander seeds, toasted
-2 tablespoons whole cardamom seeds, toasted
-1/4 cup ground turmeric
-1 tablespoon dry mustard
-1 teaspoon cayenne

In Indian cooking curry is freshly ground each day (making it far more flavorsome and pungent than the mixes sold in the store), and comes in standard and hot versions.

You can add curry powder to flavor literally any dish: meat, fish, vegetables, soups, stews, marinades, sauces and of course, curries. All curry powders differ slightly in flavor, but they can vary a lot in spiciness.

3. Berbere

This is a spice mixture whose constituent elements usually include chilli, peppers, garlic, ginger, basil, *korarima*, rue, ajwain or radhuni, nigella, and fenugreek, and sometimes it could contain rarer ingredients such as korarima and long pepper.
It serves as a key ingredient in the cuisines of Eritrea and Ethiopia.

Recipe:

-1/2 teaspoon fenugreek
-1/2 cup ground dried New Mexico chillies
-1/4 cup paprika
-1 tablespoon salt
-1 teaspoon ground ginger
-1 teaspoon onion powder
-1/8 teaspoon ground cloves
-1/2 teaspoon ground cardamom
-1/2 teaspoon ground coriander
-1/4 teaspoon ground nutmeg
-1/4 teaspoon garlic powder
-1/8 teaspoon ground cinnamon
-1/8 teaspoon ground allspice

Use when cooking densely seasoned stews and meats served with a soft, light flatbread called injera. The berbere ties everything together, using it as a dry rub for meats, a seasoning for stews, grains and lentils— even as a tableside dressing.

Here are a few useful ways to use this wonderful spice:

- Blend a can of tomato paste with honey, salt and as much berbere to your tasting. It makes the best barbecue sauce. Ever.
- Sprinkle just a bit into the cheese sauce of your favorite macaroni and cheese. The smoky, spicy change will blow you away.
- Use it directly as a dry rub for baby back ribs, steaks on the grill — or oven-roasted chicken.
- Sauté minced onions and garlic with vegetable oil, stirring in the berbere. Thin with more oil or with broth, then use as a marinade.
- Blend with softened butter then spread over hot-off-the-grill corn on the cob. Or add minced garlic and use for garlic bread.
- Add a bit to the pot when browning meat for a beef stew. Or sprinkle just a pinch over a bowl of chicken soup.
- Mix just a bit into prepared pasta sauce, or mix it directly into meatballs.
- Add a bit to ground beef when browning it for tacos.

4. Dukkah

An Egyptian mix of toasted nuts and seeds like hazelnuts, sesame seeds, coriander, and cumin.

Traditional, simple ingredients include a base of nuts such as; almonds, walnuts, pistachios, hazelnuts, cashews, pine nuts or macadamia.

Recipe:

-1/3 cup coriander seeds
-1 cup almonds
-2 teaspoons ground cumin
-1⁄2 cup sesame seeds
-1 teaspoon kosher salt
-1 teaspoon sugar
-1⁄2 teaspoon freshly ground black pepper

Method:

-In a large shallow pan, over a medium heat, roast the almonds plainly for 5–6 minutes. Remove the almonds from the pan, give them a chance to cool off for a few minutes and then finely chop them.

-Toast the sesame seeds and coriander separately, in the same pan used to toast the almonds, over a moderate heat, for 3–4 minutes or until fragrant (with a spice or coffee grinder), grind the coriander in short bursts until reasonably fine and add to a bowl along with the nuts and sesame seeds.

-Grind the cumin, sing the spice grinder or coffee grinder, or a mortar and pestle, add salt and sugar together until very fine. Taste and alter the seasoning to your own liking. Add to the sesame-nut mixture. Dukkah will keep in an airtight container for up to 4 weeks.

-It is most commonly served with pita bread that has been coated with olive oil. Then the bread is dunked into the mixture. It has a variety of uses; it can be added on meats, rice, veggies - the possibilities are endless with dukkah!

Health Benefits:

Nuts are full of healthy fats and proteins, essential for our body & brain's daily functioning and because they are so rich in goodness, you only need a few each day to give you the essential nutrients.

Dukkah is basically a great and delicious way of adding essential fats, proteins and other nutritional &medicinal properties to your food.

5. Herbes de Provence

Seasoning blends, displaying many of the herbs that grow most abundantly in the South of France.

These mixtures normally contain savory, rosemary, marjoram, oregano, thyme and other herbs.

Recipe:

-3 tablespoons dried thyme
-1 tablespoon dried oregano
-3 teaspoons dried rosemary
-2 tablespoons dried savory
-2 teaspoons dried marjoram
-1 tablespoon dried lavender flowers (optional)

Method:

-You just have to combine the herbs, and then store them an airtight container at room temperature.

-Add this prime blend of fragrant herbs, reminiscent of southern france, to tomato and vegetable dishes. Mix in with olive oil over roasted or grilled poultry, meats or seafood to savour the flavor into the cooked food. They are not often added after the cooking is complete.

Health Benefits:

Herbes de Provence are rich in antioxidants and have proven effective in managing blood pressure, insulin sensitivity, and boosting immune health. Add to that the fact they just make your food tasty and you can feel free to load up on jars full of these delicious ingredients.

6. Beau monde seasoning

In French, "beau monde" means "good society", it is a seasoning mixture. Basic versions are composed of celery powder, onion powder and salt. Some versions include additional ingredients such as garlic, clove, bay leaf, nutmeg, all spice, mace and others.

Recipe:
-1 tablespoon ground cloves
-1 tablespoon ground bay leaf
-1 1/4 teaspoons ground cinnamon
-1 tablespoon salt
-1 tablespoon ground allspice
-2 tablespoons ground pepper
-1 tablespoon ground white pepper

-1 teaspoon ground nutmeg

-1 teaspoon ground mace

-1 teaspoon celery seed

Method:

-In a small mixing bowl, mix together all ingredients. Pour into a secure jar, close it tight and store in a shady, dry place.

-It is very versatile, and can be used in almost everything from meat rubs, dips to spreads and even some cocktails.

-Beau Monde seasoning is commonly used in savory dip recipes; spring onion crème fraiche, for example. All that you usually need to do is add a tiny amount of the spice blend to a neutral base, like; sour cream or cream cheese, to create a flavorful finishing touch to sliced vegetables or crusty bread. Adding a few pinches of the seasoning (to your taste) to soups and broths can also create emphasis on the flavors without being too overpowering.

-The seasoning mix is frequently used as a dry base as well. Cooks will rub raw pieces of pork, beef or poultry in it several hours before cooking in order to seal in moisture and enhance the meat's natural juices.

7. Za'atar

A generic name for a family of related Middle Eastern herbs. It is also the name for a condiment made from the dried herb(s), mixed with sesame seeds, dried sumac, and often salt, as well as other spices. Used in Arab cuisine, both the herb and spice mixture are popular throughout the Middle East.

Recipe:

-1/4 cup sumac

-2 tablespoons thyme

-1 tablespoon roasted sesame seeds

-2 tablespoons marjoram

-2 tablespoons oregano

-1 teaspoon coarse salt

Method:

-Grind the sesame seeds in food processor or with mortar and pestle. Add remaining ingredients and mix well.

-Store za'atar in a cool, dark place in a plastic zip bag or in an airtight container. When stored properly, za'atar can be used from 3-6 months.

8. Dry Rub

A sweet and smoky barbecue rub includes; paprika, other spices and brown sugar, Kansas City style.

Recipe:

-2 cups brown sugar (see notes below)
-1/2 cup paprika
-1/4 cup + 2 tablespoons granulated garlic
-1/4 cup granulated onion
-1/4 cup mustard powder
-1/4 cup kosher salt
-1/4 cup black pepper
-1/4 cup cumin
-1/8 cup ancho or chipotle
-1/8 cup cayenne pepper

Method:
-Add all spices to your large bowl and add brown sugar. Combine it all with a whisk or you can toss all the ingredients into a large zip top bag and shake.
-There are many dry rubs styles that you can use. This is just a base mixture to get you started. If you like different things, feel free to adjust it to suit your tastes.

9. Pickling Spice

A mixture of spices used for pickling meats such as corned beef and sauerbraten are; vegetables such as onion, cabbage, and mushrooms, and fish such as; herring, salmon and trout. For pickling the spices are best left whole so the flavor cooks in, as this is the perfect solution to powdery excess that would make the liquid cloudy and unappetizing. The precise blend can vary by individual cook and manufacturer. Most include the following basic spices: bay leaves, mustard seeds (yellow or brown), and peppercorns (black, white, red, or green).

Recipe:

-2 tablespoons yellow mustard seeds
-10 bay leaves, crumbled

-1 tablespoon coriander seeds
-1 tablespoon allspice berries
-2 tablespoons black peppercorns
-1 teaspoon each of a few other spices such as: fennel seeds, dried ginger, juniper berries, mace blades, star anise, cinnamon sticks, whatever best suits your taste.

10. Poultry Spice

The basic ingredients for seasoning poultry are dried thyme and sage, which give the blend an scented, woody flavor. Other common extensions include; rosemary, marjoram, black/white pepper and we have also come across blends with parsley, savory, oregano, dried onion and garlic, seeds or celery flakes, lemon peel, nutmeg, cloves, ginger, allspice, cayenne pepper and bell pepper.

Recipe:
-1 tablespoon ground sage
-1 tablespoon ground thyme
-1 tablespoon ground marjoram
-1 teaspoon ground rosemary
-1 teaspoon crushed celery seed
-1 teaspoon ground black pepper

Method: Combine all of the ingredients and store in an sealable, compact container.

Though frequently used to season chicken, turkey and stuffing. Poultry seasoning may also be used to flavor meat or veggie burgers, pot pies, soups, and more. If you're short on time, we find that a dash of poultry seasoning is a great way to add a lot of flavor to vegetable soups and tofu marinades.

11. Citrus Dry Rub

A tasteful mix of citrus skin peel produces a citrus flavored rub that is perfect for grilling; beef, lamb, poultry, pork, or fish. Use a grater to get a fine peel and maximum flavor from each of the fruits. A grater/rasp simply reaches the outer skin and leaves the bitter pith behind offering up the true taste of oranges, limes and lemons.
Recipe:

-1 tbsp finely grated lemon zest
-3 cloves garlic, minced

-1 tbsp finely grated orange zest
-1 tbsp finely grated lime zest

-1 tbsp vegetable oil
-1 tsp chilli powder or paprika

Method:
-Stir together orange, lemon and lime peels, chilli powder, garlic and oil.
-Season to taste with salt and pepper.
-Rub mixture into the meat and let it stand for 30 minutes at room temperature or cover up and refrigerate it for up to 12 hours.

12. Dill mix

A seasoning mix combining the bright, refreshing flavor of dill with salt, onion, garlic and parsley.

Recipe:
  -2 tbsp. dill weed
  -1 tsp. dried onion powder
  -1/2 tsp. garlic powder
  -1/2 tsp. seasoning salt
  -1 tsp. dried parsley

How to use: This exclusive blend of onion, garlic, dill weed, herbs and spices is truly a multi-purpose seasoning that is excellent in; butter, dips, fish, salmon and poultry.
Infuse all of the ingredients and store in a sealable container.

13. Advieh

This aromatically warm blend comes from Persian cuisine, and it can be used in all kinds of rice dishes, meats, vegetables, and more.

Advieh is comparable to a mild Garam Masala — fragrant, a little sweet, and gently warming rather than spicy. It's also quite versatile and can be used in rice pilafs, grilled or roasted vegetables, meat or bean stews, and rice puddings. You can also sprinkle it on roasted winter squash or add a pinch to an omelette or frittata.

Although the particular combination of spices varies by region, advieh typically includes ingredients like dried rose petals or buds, cardamom, cinnamon, and cumin, all ground to a fine powder. Some recipes also include black pepper, caraway, cloves, coriander, dried lime, ginger, nutmeg, pistachio, saffron, or turmeric.

Recipe:

-1 teaspoon ground cinnamon

-1 teaspoon ground nutmeg

-1 teaspoon ground rose petals

-1 teaspoon ground cardamom

-1/2 teaspoon ground cumin

Method: Combine all spice ingredients together and put the mixture into a small jar. Store it in a cool and dry place.

14. Taco seasoning Mix

Quick and easy, tastes much better than the store bought mix. This is a great way to enjoy the savory flavor without the high amount of sodium.

Recipe:

-2 tsp instant onion, Minced

-1tsp chilli powder

-1⁄2tsp dried red pepper, Crushed

-1⁄4tsp dried oregano

-1tsp salt

-1⁄2tsp cornstarch

-1⁄2tsp instant garlic, Minced

-1⁄2tsp cumin, Ground

Method:

-First, combine all ingredients in a small bowl and blend well. Then, spoon mixture onto a 6-inch square of aluminium foil and fold to make airtight. Store in a cool, dry place and use within 6 months.

15. Fine Herbs

A blend of four fresh herbs, the main one is chervil. Traditionally, the other three herbs are; chives, tarragon, and parsley and they always come fresh. Combine equal proportions of each herb and mince them as fine as possible. When cooking, add the herbs toward the end so that the flavor is still fresh and bright.

I can use this combination of herbs in vinaigrettes for simple summer salads or in herb butter for sandwiches. The tarragon, in particular, adds an unexpected licorice flavor.

16. Khmeli suneli

This is a complex and fragrant mixture of warm, nutty, grassy, and bitter flavors.

The combination of ingredients varies between households and spice merchants but khmeli suneli commonly contains:

-fenugreek seeds and leaves

-coriander

-savory

-black peppercorns

Method: Other additions may include dill, bay leaves, mint, and dried marigold petals. You can also use cassia and cloves.

Traditionally used in stews and meat dishes, khmeli suneli also provides amazing depth of flavor to beans and roasted vegetables.

17. Quatre Epices

Meaning "four spices," this French blend typically includes ground black and/or white pepper, cloves, nutmeg, and ginger. This recipe is commonly used to season forcemeats for sausages and terrines, and it should be considered a suggestion; quantities and proportions given are typical but not written in stone. Vary the amounts to suit your own palate.

Recipe:

-2 tablespoons (1/8 cup) white peppercorns

-1/4 teaspoon freshly grated nutmeg

-1/2 teaspoon (about 12) whole cloves

-1/4 teaspoon ground ginger-

18. Chaat Masala

Chaat masala is a spice blend consisting of black salt, chilli powder, cumin seeds and dry mango powder. That is why traditional combinations are home ground and kept ready for use.

<u>Recipe:</u>
- -1 cup slightly roasted coriander (dhania) seeds
- -1 cup whole dry kashmiri red chillies, roasted
- -1 cup roasted cumin seeds (jeera)
- -1 cup dried mango powder (amchur)
- -3 tbsp black peppercorns (kalimirch)
- -1 cup salt
- -3 tbsp black salt (sanchal)

<u>Method:</u> Powder all the ingredients together in a grinder. Store it into an sealed container. Use as required.

19. Garam Masala

Garam Masala is the Indian equivalent of French herbes de Provence or Chinese five-spice powder. The recipe changes from region to region within northern India and can be varied according to whim. Here, rosebuds (found in Indian or Middle Eastern markets) add an exciting floral note, but you can substitute black cardamom, fennel seeds (in the style of Kashmir), or a teaspoon of royal cumin (shahi or kala zeera, also found in Indian markets)—or just eliminate the roses altogether. Once you taste the difference that this simple powder makes in your cooking, you will find it worth the investment of cupboard space. As a rule (one that certainly gets broken at times), Garam Masala is only added at the last step of cooking, almost like a fresh herb, because it tends to become bitter if cooked too long.

<u>Recipe:</u>
- -1 tablespoon dried miniature rosebuds (optional)
- -A 1-inch piece cinnamon stick, broken into pieces
- -2 bay leaves
- -1/4 cup cumin seeds
- -1/3 cup coriander seeds
- -1 tablespoon green cardamom pods
- -1 tablespoon whole black peppercorns
- -2 teaspoons whole cloves
- -1 dried red chillies

-1/4 teaspoon freshly grated nutmeg

-1/8 teaspoon ground mace

Method:

-If the roses have stems, break them off and discard. Heat the roses with the cinnamon, bay leaves, cumin seeds, coriander seeds, cardamom pods, whole peppercorns, cloves, and chillies in a medium skillet over medium-high heat, stirring often, until the cumin becomes brown, 2 1/2 to 3 minutes. Transfer to a spice grinder or coffee mill, add the nutmeg and mace, and grind until powder fine. Store in an airtight container for up to 4 months.

20. Panch Phoron

A Bengali five-spice blend of whole fenugreek, nigella, cumin, black mustard, and fennel seeds. This five spice mix is so easy to make yet adds tremendous flavor and aroma to Bengali dishes and anything else you can think of.
Most spice mixes are ground, and depending on how many spices constitute the blend, you might be running your spice grinder or pounding your mortar and pestle for a very long time! This one is simple: just five spices, used whole.

While there are some variations, the spices in Bengali panch phoron are generally cumin seeds, fennel seeds, fenugreek seeds, black mustard seeds, and nigella (also known as kalonji) seeds. (All of these should be available at Indian markets and good spice shops.)

Mix together an equal quantity of each spice and store in an airtight container. To use panch phoron, fry the spices in oil or ghee until they "pop" — this releases the aroma and bittersweet, anise-y flavor of the blend. Add your vegetables or meat to the pan, or simply toss the panch phoron into other dishes. I like using a tablespoon or so of panch phoron with broccoli, cauliflower, roasted potatoes, and lentils. To use in pickles, I simply toast the spices in a dry pan without oil.

21. Jerk Spice Blend (Dry)

Jerk is a style of cooking native to Jamaica in which meat is dry-rubbed or wet marinated with a very hot spice mixture called Jamaican jerk spice.
Jerk seasoning is commonly applied to pork and chicken. Modern recipes also apply jerk spice mixes to fish, shrimp, shellfish, beef, sausage, lamb, and tofu.

From merely hot to incendiary, this Caribbean jerk seasoning gets its kick from a blend of ingredients such as chillies, thyme, cinnamon, garlic, and nutmeg.

Recipe:
  - -1 tablespoon garlic powder
  - -2 to 3 teaspoons cayenne pepper
  - -2 teaspoons onion powder
  - -2 teaspoons dried thyme
  - -2 teaspoons dried parsley
  - -2 teaspoons sugar
  - -2 teaspoons salt
  - -1 teaspoon paprika
  - -1 teaspoon ground allspice
  - -1/2 teaspoon black pepper
  - -1/2 teaspoon dried crushed red pepper
  - -1/2 teaspoon ground nutmeg
  - -1/4 teaspoon ground cinnamon

Method: All you have to do is to combine all ingredients, then store the blend in an airtight container for up to 3 months.

22. Adobo

An all-purpose seasoning that contains garlic, oregano, pepper, and other spices; used in Mexican and other Latin American cuisines.

Adobo is the immersion of raw food in a stock (or sauce) composed variously of paprika, oregano, salt, garlic, and vinegar to preserve and enhance its flavor. The Portuguese alternative is known as Carne de Vinha d' Alhos.

The practice is native to Iberia, namely Spanish cuisine and Portuguese cuisine. It was widely adopted in Latin America and other Spanish and Portuguese colonies, including the Azores and Madeira.

Adobo was employed initially as a method of food preservation, but in time—with the advent of refrigeration methods—it came to be used first as a method of adding flavour to foods before cooking.

Recipe:

- -2 tablespoons salt
- -1 tablespoon paprika
- -2 teaspoons ground black pepper
- -1 1⁄2 teaspoons onion powder
- -1 1⁄2 teaspoons dried oregano
- -1 1⁄2 teaspoons ground cumin
- -1 teaspoon garlic powder
- -1 teaspoon chilli powder

Method: In a bowl, stir together the salt, paprika, black pepper, onion powder, oregano, cumin, garlic powder, and chilli powder.
Store it in a sealed jar in a cool, dry place.

23. Bahārāt Spice Blend

Bahārāt is a spice mixture or blend used in Middle Eastern cuisine, especially in the Mashriq area, as well as in Turkish, Iranian, Kurdish and Israeli cuisine.

The mixture of finely ground spices is often used to season lamb, fish, chicken, beef, and soups and may be used as a condiment.

Typical ingredients of baharat may include: Allspice, Black peppercorns, Cardamom seeds, Cassia bark, Cloves, Coriander seeds, Cumin seeds, Nutmeg, Dried red chilli peppers or paprika.

Turkish baharat includes mint as the modal ingredient. In Tunisia, baharat refers to a simple mixture of dried rosebuds and ground cinnamon, often combined with black pepper. In the Arab states of the Persian Gulf, loomi (dried black lime) and saffron may also be used for the kebsa spice mixture (also called "Gulf baharat").

Recipe:
- -3 parts coriander seeds
- -3 parts cinnamon
- -4 parts black pepper
- -3 parts cloves
- -4 parts cumin seeds
- -3 parts nutmeg
- -1 part cardamom pods
- -6 parts paprika

Method:

-The mixture can be rubbed into meat or mixed with olive oil and lime juice to form a marinade.

24. Pumpkin Spice Blend

This spice is a blend of "warm" spices. For a delicious spice to add to pumpkin pie, try this spice blend. The blend can also be added to spiced nut blends.

Typically ingredients are: cinnamon, nutmeg, cloves, allspice and mace. Pumpkin pie spice adds a nice extra "pumpkin" taste to pumpkin pie.

Recipe:
  -1/2 tsp ground cinnamon
  -1/4 tsp ground ginger
  -1/8 tsp ground allspice
  -1/8 tsp ground nutmeg

Method: Combine all ingredients. Store in an airtight container.

25. Harissa

Harissa is a Tunisian hot chilli pepper paste whose main ingredients are roasted red peppers, serrano peppers and other hot chilli peppers and spices and herbs such as garlic paste, coriander seed, or caraway as well as some vegetable or olive oil for preservation. It is most closely associated with Tunisia, Libya and Algeria but recently also making inroads into Morocco according to Moroccan food expert Paula Wolfert.

As with the European cuisine, chilli peppers were imported into Maghrebian cuisine via the Columbian Exchange, presumably during the Spanish occupation of Tunisia between 1535 and 1574.

Recipes for harissa vary according to the household and region. Variations can include the addition of cumin, red peppers, garlic, coriander, and lemon juice. In Saharan regions, harissa can have a smoky flavor.

Harissa is sometimes described as "Tunisia's main condiment", even "the national condiment of Tunisia", or at least as "the hallmark of Tunisia's fish and meat dishes". In Tunisia, harissa is used as an ingredient in a meat (goat or lamb) or fish stew with vegetables, and as a flavoring for couscous. It is also used for lablabi, a chickpea soup usually eaten for breakfast.

In Algeria, harissa is commonly added to soups, stews, and couscous.

In some European countries it is used sometimes as a breakfast spread for tartines or rolls.

Harissa paste can also be used as a rub for meat or eggplants.

In Israel, harissa is a common topping for sabich and shawarma, although other hot sauces like the Yemeni zhug or the Iraqi amba are also employed.

Recipe:
    -2 tsp cumin seeds
    -2 tsp coriander seeds
    -4 tbsp dried red chillies, chopped
    -2 tsp mild paprika powder
    -1 tsp sea salt
    -1 tsp caraway seeds, ground
    -1 tsp mint, dried
    -1 tsp garlic flakes, dried
    -some water
    -some olive oil, extra virgin

Method:
    - Dry-roast and then grind the cumin and coriander seeds.
    -Mix all the dry ingredients together.

How to prepare for use:
    -Mix the blend, as much as you need, with an equal amount of water, then just enough oil to create the consistency you desire.
    -Store the unused dry mix in an air-tight container.

26. Ras El Hanout

Ras el hanout or Rass el hanout is a spice mix from North Africa. It plays a similar role in North African cuisine as garam masala does in Indian cuisine.

Ras el hanout is used in many savory dishes, sometimes rubbed on meat or fish, or stirred into couscous or rice. The mix is generally associated with Morocco, although neighboring North African countries use it as well.

There is no definitive composition of spices that makes up ras el hanout. Each shop, company, or family may have their own blend. The mixture usually consists of over a dozen spices, in different proportions, although some purists insist that it must contain exactly 12 items. Commonly used ingredients include cardamom, cumin, clove, cinnamon, nutmeg, mace, allspice, dry ginger, chilli peppers, coriander seed, peppercorn, sweet and hot paprika, fenugreek, and dry turmeric. Some spices may be particular to the region, such as ash berries, chufa, grains of paradise, orris root, monk's pepper, cubebs, dried rosebud, fennel seed or aniseed, galangal, long pepper. Ingredients may be toasted before being ground or pounded in a mortar and mixed together. Some preparations include salt or sugar, but that is generally not the accepted practice.

<u>Recipe:</u>
- -2 teaspoons ground nutmeg
- -2 teaspoons ground coriander
- -2 teaspoons ground cumin
- -2 teaspoons ground ginger
- -2 teaspoons turmeric
- -2 teaspoons salt
- -2 teaspoons cinnamon
- -1 1⁄2 teaspoons sugar
- -1 1⁄2 teaspoons paprika
- -1 1⁄2 teaspoons ground black pepper
- -1 teaspoon cayenne pepper
- -1 teaspoon cardamom powder
- -1 teaspoon ground allspice
- -1⁄2 teaspoon ground cloves--

<u>Method:</u> Mix all the spices together. Store in an airtight container.

27. Five-spice powder

Five-spice powder is a spice mixture of five spices, used primarily in Chinese cuisine but also used in other Asian and Arabic cookery.

While there are many variants, a common mix is: Star anise, Cloves, Chinese Cinnamon, Sichuan pepper, Fennel seeds. Other recipes may contain anise seed or ginger root, nutmeg, turmeric, Amomum villosum pods, Amomum cardamomum pod, licorice, Mandarin orange peel or galangal.

In South China, Cinnamomum loureiroi and Mandarin orange peel is commonly used as a substitute for Cinnamomum cassia and cloves, respectively, producing a different flavour for southern five-spice powders.

Five-spice may be used with fatty meats such as pork, duck or goose. It is used as a spice rub for chicken, duck, pork and seafood, in red cooking recipes, or added to the breading for fried foods. Five-spice is used in recipes for Cantonese roasted duck, as well as beef stew. It is used as a marinade for Vietnamese broiled chicken. The five-spice powder mixture has followed the Chinese diaspora and has been incorporated into other national cuisines throughout Asia.

Although this mixture is used in restaurant cooking, many Chinese households do not use it in day-to-day cooking. In Hawaii, some restaurants place a shaker of the spice on each patron's table. A seasoned salt can be easily made by dry-roasting common salt with five-spice powder under low heat in a dry pan until the spice and salt are well mixed.

Recipe:
   -1 teaspoon ground cinnamon
   -1 teaspoon ground cloves
   -1 teaspoon fennel seed, toasted and ground
   -1 teaspoon ground star anise
   -1 teaspoon szechuan peppercorns, toasted and ground

Method: Mix the spices together and store in an airtight jar.

28. Gomashio

Gomashio is a dry side dressing, similar to furikake, made from unhulled sesame seeds and salt. It is often used in Japanese cuisine, such as a topping for sekihan.
It is can also be sprinkled over plain rice or onigiri. Some commercially sold gomashio also has sugar mixed in with the salt.

The sesame seeds used to make gomashio may be either tan or black in color. They are toasted before being mixed in with the salt. Occasionally the salt is also toasted. The ratio of sesame seeds to salt varies according to taste and diet, generally ranging between 5:1 and 15:1.
Gomashio is often homemade, though it is also commercially available in glass or plastic packaging.

Recipe:

2 cups unhulled brown sesame seeds

-3 tablespoons sea salt

Method:

-In a heavy skillet (cast iron is best), toast salt until it turns a grey color. Set aside.

-Toast the 2 cups sesame seeds, stirring constantly, till they start popping and turn a nice brown.

-Watch them closely, or they will burn!

-The traditional way to grind them is with a mortar and pestle, just until the seeds crack open and release their oils.

-The texture should be light and sandy.

-They should ultimately be 95% crushed.

-Store gomasio in a tightly closed glass jar, keep in a cool dry place.

29. Nori Shake Blend

This tasty Nori Shake was greatly influenced by a recipe from Mark Bittman, in his incredible cookbook 'How to Cook Everything Vegetarian'. His books are so stellar because he packs them with recipes, but also includes the theory and the 'know how' that is needed in order for you to create your own recipes. This "Shake" is delicious on pretty much everything. When the seaweed meets anything hot (think steamed rice, sautéed veggies or hot pasta) it sticks in the most delightful way, infusing the food with a salty, spicy, nutty kick. Not to mention the nutrition blast you are getting from the seaweed, that otherwise might be tough to sneak into your diet.

Recipe:

-2 full sized sheets of nori seaweed (the kind used for sushi wrappers)

-2 dried hot chilli peppers (or about 1 Tbsp chilli flakes)

-1/8 cup sesame seeds

Method:

-Heat a skillet or shallow pan on the stove until it is pretty hot, then set at medium high heat.

-Place the sheets of seaweed in the skillet to toast. Move it around briskly so that it doesn't stick to the pan. As the seaweed heats up, it will turn a brighter green and become more brittle. When the sheets have turned bright green, remove from heat.

-While the pan is still hot, add the sesame seeds and toast for about a minute, or until they are browned. They will want to hop out of the pan—so watch yourself! A lid may be in order.

-Put the toasted seaweed, sesame seeds, and chillies (spice it to your taste) in a blender or a food processor and blend until the mixture is coarsely chopped.

-That's it! Put the shake in a covered container and keep it in the refrigerator. It should keep for about 2 weeks.

30. Greek Seasoning

This is a quick and easy way to add a great Greek flavor to most anything you want to cook. Try combining this seasoning with olive oil and lemon juice to make a great marinade. Use when any recipe calls for Greek seasoning.

Recipe:
  -2 tablespoons/30 ml dried oregano
  -5 teaspoons/25 mL onion powder
  -5 teaspoons/25 mL garlic powder
  -1 tablespoon/15 mL salt
  -1 tablespoon/15 mL fresh ground black pepper
  -1 tablespoon/15 mL beef-flavored bouillon granules
  -1 tablespoon/15 mL dried parsley
  -1 teaspoon/5 mL ground cinnamon
  -1 teaspoon/5 mL ground nutmeg

Method: Combine all ingredients and store in an airtight container. Keep in a cool, dark place.

31. Lemon Pepper Spice Mix

Lemon pepper is a popular ingredient in many recipes.
It is perfect on chicken, a burger or pasta.

Recipe:
- 1 or 2 tablespoon lemon zest, about 3 lemons
- 2 or 3 tablespoons black pepper
- 1 tablespoon sea salt

Method:
- Preheat toaster oven to lowest setting.
- In a large bowl, combine lemon zest and black pepper. Cover metal pan fitted for toaster oven with foil and spread mixture evenly in pan. Allow to bake low and slow until zest is completely dried. Mine took about 26-30 minutes.
- Transfer lemon-pepper mixture to a bowl. Using the back of a spoon (or spice grinder if you have one), crush mixture until desired texture is achieved. Mix in salt, 1 tsp at a time. Continue to add salt until you have the right balance to fit your taste.
- Depending on size of lemons, you may need more lemons.
- If you want more of a lemon taste, reduce pepper or add more lemon zest.
- Seasoning may be kept in an air tight container for a few months.

32. Apple Pie Spice

This Apple Pie Spice Mix is the perfect substitute to the traditional Apple Pie, Apple Crumble, Homemade Apple Butter, and other Baked Apple Recipes. You may also use this to flavor other pastries, cookies, and cakes.

Recipe:
- 4 teaspoons ground
- Cinnamon
- 4 teaspoons ground coriander
- 1/2 teaspoon ground nutmeg
- 1/2 teaspoon ground allspice
- 1/2 teaspoon ground ginger
- 1/4 teaspoon ground cloves
- 1/4 teaspoon ground cardamom

Method: Combine all ingredients in a small jar, shake well. Store in airtight container.

33. Colombo Curry Powder

Colombo curry powder is pungent and aromatic. Making your own gives you control to adjust amounts to your own liking.

This spice mixture is similar to regular curry powder. However, Colombo powder contains one unusual ingredient: roasted uncooked rice. This technique gives the powder a nutty taste and makes the rice easier to grind. The rice also acts as a natural thickener when cooking, which makes it great for soups and stews. Colombo powder is consumed mostly in the French West Indies (Guadeloupe, Martinique, St. Martin and Saint Barthélemy (St. Barts) and the smaller islands of Les Saintes, Marie-Galante, and La Désirade).

However, since its origins are Indian, it's also an ingredient in Jamaican and Trinidadian recipes. The spice mixture is also called, 'Poudre de Colombo' or West Indian curry powder. You can use Colombo powder in any recipe that you would use curry powder. Spice up meats, poultry, or vegetables.

Recipe:
- -1/4 cup uncooked white rice
- -1/4 cup cumin seeds
- -1/4 cup coriander seeds
- -1 tablespoon black mustard seeds (yellow or brown will due)
- -1 tablespoon black peppercorns
- -1 tablespoon fenugreek seeds
- -1 teaspoon whole cloves
- -1/4 cup turmeric

Method:
- -Toast the rice over medium heat in a dry skillet until a lightly golden.
- -Shake the pan often to prevent burning. This will take about 5 minutes.
- -Transfer the rice to a plate or platter to cool.
- -Place the remaining spices, except the turmeric, into the skillet and cook over medium heat until fragrant and toasty.
- -Shake the pan often to prevent burning. This will take about 3 minutes.
- -Transfer the mixture to a plate or platter to cool.

34. Fajita Seasoning Mix

Rather than buying fajita seasoning, it's easy to make your own. Approximately 2 tablespoons equals 1 store-bought seasoning packet.

Recipe:
- -1 tablespoon cornstarch
- -2 teaspoons chilli powder
- -1 teaspoon salt
- -1 teaspoon paprika
- -1 teaspoon sugar
- -3⁄4 teaspoon crushed chicken bouillon cube
- -1⁄2 teaspoon onion powder
- -1⁄4 teaspoon garlic powder
- -1⁄4 teaspoon cayenne pepper
- -1⁄4 teaspoon cumin

Method:
-Combine all ingredients in a small bowl.
-Use as needed in recipes calling for fajita seasoning. Yield - 10 teaspoons.

35. Scottish Mixed Spice

This delicious spice mix is used to bake cakes and breads and you can also sprinkle it into your oatmeal.

Recipe:
- -4 teaspoons ground ginger
- -2 teaspoons ground nutmeg
- -2 teaspoons ground black pepper
- -2 teaspoons ground allspice
- -2 teaspoons ground cinnamon
- -2 teaspoons ground cloves

Method: Mix all ingredients together and store in an air-tight container.

36. Gyros Spice Mix

You can use this mix on whole or cut up pieces of meat.
If the chilli powder seems too hot for you, leave it out, it will still be a nice spice mix.
When making a marinade with small pieces of meat you should add fresh cut up coriander leaves. Marinating time can take 20 minutes or up to a day.
Together with the lemon juice you can also use buttermilk or yogurt.

Recipe:
-   -2 tablespoons chilli powder
    -   -1 tablespoon ground coriander
    -   -1 tablespoon ground cumin
    -   -1/2 tablespoon paprika, hot or sweet
    -   -1/2 tablespoon garlic powder
    -   -1 tablespoon dried parsley
    -   -2 teaspoons dried oregano
    -   -2 teaspoons dried thyme
    -   -1 teaspoon ground cinnamon

Method:
-Mix herbs and spices, transfer to a jar.
-Use for chicken, lamb, pork and minced/ground meats.
-Mix a few teaspoons with lemon/lime juice, olive oil and salt to taste and mix that with the type of meat you selected.
-For kebabs or burgers, add some salt to the mince.

37. Argentinean Chimichurri

It's an Argentinean sauce or condiment, similar to pesto, which is popular throughout South America.
This basic version uses fresh parsley, oregano, garlic, oil and vinegar and a little bit of chilli pepper, though the variations on this theme are endless.
In Argentina it is used both as a marinade and a sauce for grilled steak, but you can use it also with fish, chicken, or even pasta.

Recipe:
-   -1 cup firmly packed fresh flat-leaf parsley, trimmed of thick stems
    3-4 garlic cloves.

-2 Tbsps fresh oregano leaves (can sub 2 teaspoons dried oregano)

-1/2 cup olive oil

-2 Tbsp red or white wine vinegar

-1 teaspoon sea salt

-1/4 teaspoon freshly ground black pepper

-1/4 teaspoon red pepper flakes

Method:

- Chop the parsley finely, fresh oregano, and garlic (or process in a food processor several pulses). Place in a small bowl.

-Stir in the olive oil, vinegar, salt, pepper, and red pepper flakes. Adjust seasonings.

-Serve immediately or refrigerate. If chilled, return to room temperature before serving. Can keep for a day or two.

38. Thai Green Chicken Curry

The Thai word for Green Curry actually translates to "Sweet Green Curry", but that doesn't imply that this dish is sweet. Instead, "sweet green" means "light green" in Thai.

While the idea of making curry from scratch may be initially daunting, nothing could be further from the truth. This curry paste has quite a few ingredients, but all you do is basically throw them all together and purée; the paste will keep for a month in the fridge and there's enough paste to make three curries. Making the actual curry is even easier – it's a 20-minute meal, if not less.

Recipe:

-1 handful chopped cilantro leaves and stems (about 1/2 cup)

-1 handful chopped thai basil leaves (about 1/2 cup)

-2 jalapeño peppers, stems, seeds, and ribs removed, sliced

-1 stick lemon grass, white part only (about 3″ total), thinly sliced

-1″ fresh galangal (ginger okay), peeled and sliced

-2 large shallots, coarsely chopped

-4 cloves garlic, coarsely chopped

-1 green cardamom pod

-1 tsp shrimp paste

-1 tsp fish sauce

-1 tsp salt

-1/2 tsp ground coriander

-1/2 tsp ground cumin

-1/2 tsp white pepper

-juice and zest of one lime (2 tbsp juice, 1 tsp zest)

Method:

-In a food processor or blender, process all of the curry paste ingredients together into a smooth paste. Add water if needed, but the shallots may release enough liquid on their own. If the paste becomes too soupy, strain it into a bowl to separate the liquid and the paste.

-You'll then want to add the liquid to the curry when you add the first coconut milk. If you're up for a challenge, you can make the paste in the traditional manner – with a mortar, pestle, and some elbow grease. The curry paste can be made ahead and stored in the fridge for up to a month.

39. Piri-Piri or Peri-Peri Spice Mix

In Spain and Portugal, piri-piri or peri-peri are used as generic terms for hot sauces and chili powders used for barbecue. This recipe is smoky and hot, with a bitter-sour hint of lemon peel. A nice, tangy and very mild hot sauce that you will enjoy.

Recipe:
  -2 tablespoons smoked paprika
  -1 teaspoon cayenne pepper
  -1 teaspoon garlic powder
  -3/4 teaspoon salt
  -1/2 teaspoon ground black pepper
  -1/2 teaspoon lemon peel
  -1/2 teaspoon ground oregano

Method:

Combine all ingredients in small bowl. Store it in airtight container.

40. Carrabba's Bread Dip

The herb combination is great for a tasty appetizer.

Recipe:
  -1 Tbsp crushed red pepper flakes
  -1 Tbsp crushed black pepper
  -1 Tbsp dried oregano

-1 Tbsp dried rosemary

-1 Tbsp dried basil

-1 Tbsp dried parsley

-1 Tbsp minced garlic

-2 tsp garlic salt

Method:

-In a container with a lid, combine all the ingredients together. Store mixture in the refrigerator until needed.

-Put 1 tbsp of mixture per person into a shallow saucer with raised edges. Pour virgin olive oil over the mixture, and dip warm sourdough or French bread into the mixture.

41. Savory Herb Rub

A quick and easy savory herb rub that is perfect for gift giving or adding a medley of flavor to your pork, chicken, lamb or fish.

Recipe:

-2 tbsp Garlic powder

-1/4 cup Lemon peel, dried

-2 tbsp Onion, dried

-2/3 cup Parsley, dried

-1/4 cup Rosemary, dried

-1/3 cup Thyme, dried

-1/4 cup Black pepper, coarse ground

-1 1/3 cups Kosher salt or coarse sea salt

Method:

-In a medium bowl, stir together salt, parsley, thyme, rosemary, lemon peel, pepper, garlic powder and onion. Divide mixture among 1/2 cup glass jars or gift tines, stirring occasionally as you spoon.

-Cover and label jars or tins and add hang tags with directions for use.

-Instructions for use as a rub:

-Lightly brush pork, chicken, lamb or fish with olive oil. Tub the herb mixture evenly over all sides of meat, poultry or fish. Let stand for 15 minutes, then grill or roast the meat.

42. Bo-Kaap Cape Malay Curry Powder Mix

Influenced by Malay cuisine, (Cape/Malay) curry powder/ masala is a blend of sweet and pungent spices that includes; cloves, cardamon, fennel, mustard, coriander, turmeric, fenugreek, a little chilli and black pepper. A curry powder/masala of a mild heat yet that is full of the flavors you expect in an Indian curry. This curry spice mix is wonderful in all types of curries, but especially authentic Cape Malay style cuisine.

Recipe:
- 1 tablespoon clove
- 1/2 cup coriander seed
- 1 tablespoon fennel seed
- 1 tablespoon black mustard seeds
- 3 tablespoons fenugreek seeds
- 2 tablespoons black peppercorns
- 3 small dried hot red chilies, seeds and stems removed
- 3 tablespoons cumin seeds
- 1/4 cup ground cardamom
- 1/4 cup ground turmeric
- 1 tablespoon ground ginger
- 2 curry leaves, chopped into small pieces

Method:
- Place all the whole seeds in a frying pan and dry roast for a minute or two, until they become pungent and release their fragrance. Place them in a food processor or coffee grinder and pulse until they are finely ground - or grind them with a pestle and mortar.
- Add the remaining ground spices, including the chillies and the curry leaves, to the roasted spices and mix well.
- Store in an airtight jar or tin for up to 6 months, in a dry, cool and dark place.

43. Garlic Bread Seasoning

It is typically used on a baguette which is partially sliced downwards, allowing the condiments to soak into the loaf while keeping it in one piece. The bread is then stuffed through the cuts with oil and minced garlic before baking. Alternatively, butter and garlic powder are used, or the bread is cut lengthwise into separate slices which are individually garnished.

Recipe:
- 1/2 cup powdered parmesan cheese
- 2 teaspoons kosher salt
- 2 tablespoons garlic powder
- 2 teaspoons oregano
- 2 teaspoons basil

-2 teaspoons marjoram

-2 teaspoons parsley

Method:

-Combine ingredients and store in an air tight container in the fridge. Will keep up to 3 months.

-Brush the bread sticks with melted butter when they came out of the oven and then sprinkle them with this seasoning.

-Another way to use it: combine 1 1/2 Tablespoons with 1/2 cup room temperature butter, spread on French bread.

44. Mulling Spice Mix

This is a recipe for mulling spices; it works well with apple cider or wine or other festive drinks. Bags of this mulling spice also make wonderful gifts! It can even be boiled on the stovetop as a nice spicy potpourri or put together a gift basket of the spices, with some fresh apple cider, tea and/or a bottle of red wine to share.

Recipe:

-4 organic whole nutmeg

-1/2 cup organic cardamom pods

-1/2 cup organic cinnamon chips (sweet)

-1/4 cup organic orange peel

-1/4 cup organic lemon peel

-1/4 cup organic ginger root

-1/4 cup organic whole cloves

-1/4 cup organic whole allspice berries

-2 organic vanilla beans

-organic star anise, whole pods (optional)

-organic cinnamon sticks (sweet)

Method:

-Put nutmeg and cardamom pods in a thick plastic or cloth bag and whack with a mallet or heavy rolling pin to break into pieces. You can also do this in a food processor or spice grinder, but don't grind too fine.

-Put nutmeg and cardamom pieces in a bowl and add the cinnamon chips, ginger root, orange and lemon peel, allspice berries, and cloves. Scrape the inside of vanilla beans and add to this spice mixture (you can save the vanilla pods for homemade vanilla extract or to infuse sugar or honey).

-This makes about 2 1/2 cups–enough mulling spices for several recipes. You can put about 1/4 cup in a cotton drawstring bag or wrap in cheesecloth and tie well. Toss in 1-2 star anise pods per bag, if you'd like. Suspend the cinched or tied bag in the wine, cider or punch.

45. Sambhar Spice Blend

Every curry has its own spice blend. Sambhar is a curry made from lentil, coconut or/and vegetables. This is a spice blend for that curry. It is usually enjoyed with a hot cup of steaming rice and a dollop of ghee. It can also be enjoyed with dosa (a lentil crêpe) or idli (rice pan cakes). The taste is spicy, tangy, balanced with a hint of sweetness.

Recipe:
- -1 tbsp cumin/jeera
- -1 tsp oil
- -1/2 tsp peppercorn/kala mirch
- -5 or 6 red chilli (whole)/ laal mirch
- -4 tbsp coriander seed/dhaniya beej
- -1/2 tsp fenugreek seed/methi beej (optional)
- -1 tbsp gram lentil/chana daal
- -1/4 tbsp cinnamon stick (broken)/dalchini
- -1/4 tsp asafoetida
- -handful of dry coconut powder or fresh coconut

Method:

-Roast all of the ingredients in oil (except the coconut), until you smell the aroma. Then wait for it to cool. Add the dry coconut powder and dry grind OR you can add the fresh coconut and make a paste.

46. Medieval Spice Blend

Here is the recipe for the simple spice blend the medieval Europeans would use, from England to Romania, and everywhere in between.
For warmth, a combination of cinnamon, clove, nutmeg and/or mace were often included, usually not altogether. And grains of paradise were utilized as a daily ingredient. Harder to find now, you can use their cousin the simple black peppercorn in place. Use on chicken, foul, game, fish, soups, stews, or vegetables. Add salt to taste.

Recipe:
- -6 Tbsp ground ginger
- -4 Tbsp granulated white sugar
- -3 Tbsp ground cinnamon
- -2 tsp whole cloves
- -2 tsp whole black pepper corns

Method:

-Place all of the spices into a grinder and pulse until finely ground into a powder. Keep in an airtight container (preferably made of glass) for up to a month.

47. Maple Garlic Pepper Rub

There's something so perfect about the sweet and salty, peppery, garlicky rub. It delivers just enough of each of the components without being too much of any of its parts. This rub is beyond delicious on chicken and pork whether pan-fried, roasted, broiled, or grilled.

Recipe:
-1/2 cup pure maple sugar
-2 tablespoons kosher salt
-1 tablespoon granulated garlic
-1 tablespoon cracked or coarsely ground black pepper

Method:

-Mix all ingredients together and store in a cool, dark place in an airtight jar.

48. Tabil Blend

A potent, versatile Tunisian spice blend made of coriander and caraway seeds, chili flakes, and garlic. You can use tabil as a seasoning or dry rub for meats and vegetables.

Recipe:
-1/3 cup coriander seeds
-1 tablespoon caraway seeds
-1 tablespoon red pepper flakes
-1 tablespoon garlic powder

Method:
-Toast the coriander seeds, caraway seeds, and pepper flakes in a dry skillet over medium heat until fragrant (about 2 minutes). Transfer the spices to a container to cool slightly.
-While the mixture is still warm, add the garlic powder and mix well. Once the mixture has cooled to room temperature, blitz it in a spice grinder.

-Store the tabil in a sealed container and stick it in a cool, dark, dry place, and it'll last for a long, long time.

49. Haitian Epices Blend

This recipe for Epices (Haitian Seasoning), by Tracy J. - Ancillary, is from ear, nose and throat South Florida family cookbook. It works great on Soups, Stews, Salads and Sauces.

Recipe:
- -3 Green Bell Peppers 4 sticks of Thyme
- -2 Red Bell Peppers
- -1 pack of HOT Jamaican Peppers
- -3 bunches of Fresh Parsley 1/3 container of seasoned salt
- -4 bunches of Scallions
- -2 1/2 Tbsp. Sugar
- -2 1/2 packets of Peeled Garlic
- -1 1/3 Cup Olive Oil
- -1 Tbsp. Cloves

Note: HOT Peppers are optional!

Method:
-Clean scallions and parsley thoroughly. Cut bell peppers into manageable pieces and remove the heart with all the seeds. Prep all remaining ingredients.
-The olive oil should be added slowly throughout the entire blending process.
-Place food processor on medium/high speed and add the parsley first. Once parsley is all chopped and blended into a paste, you can slowly add the bell peppers, scallions, garlic interchangeably. Next, add the thyme, hot peppers and seasoned salt. After everything is blended, stir sugar into mixture.
-Now you're done and you place mixture into container or you can begin to season your food.
It can be stored in the refrigerator for months.

50. Dry Spice Rub for Pork Ribs

Lots of spices and brown sugar join allows you to make a sweet and savory dry rub for pork ribs.

Recipe:
- -1 tablespoon paprika
- -1 teaspoon ground black pepper
- -2 tablespoons brown sugar

-1 teaspoon salt
-1⁄2 teaspoon red chili flakes
-1 tablespoon garlic powder
-1 teaspoon dry ground mustard
-1 teaspoon cumin
-1⁄2 teaspoon chili powder
-1 teaspoon onion powder
-1 teaspoon steak seasoning
-1 teaspoon dry parsley

Method:
-Combine all ingredients in a bowl. Rub over pork ribs.
-Save unused dry rub in an air-tight container.

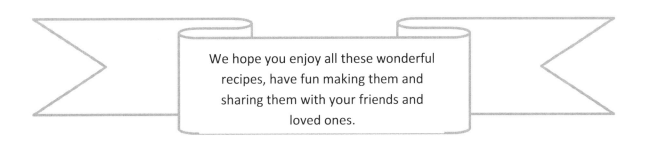

We hope you enjoy all these wonderful recipes, have fun making them and sharing them with your friends and loved ones.

Conclusion

Making your own homemade spice and herb blends are tremendously beneficial, not just in flavour but also for your health as many mixes bought from the shop contain lots of additives and chemicals. Whereas, making your own is healthy and can fit to your tastes and preferences.

There is a wide variety of blends that go well together and I hope the recipes in this eBook were helpful. There's a blend for every type of dish. You will soon eat the cuisine of every country, as every spice is unique and an acquired taste for people of different countries. I hope you will soon test and try these blends for yourself and transform your dishes to be more flavoursome and adventurous.